A GIFT TO REMEMBER

A GIFT TO REMEMBER

Written by
MERIDETH TULLOUS

Illustrated by
YLBER CËRVADIKU

A GIFT TO REMEMBER

Cover design and illustrations by Ylber Cërvadiku

Library of Congress Control Number: 2020908452

Hardcover ISBN   978-1-7349514-0-0
Paperback ISBN   978-1-7349514-1-7
Ebook ISBN   978-1-7349514-2-4

Published by H&E Press
Fort Worth, TX

H&E PRESS

To my sweet boys,
Eldon and Hudson, for writing an
unselfish letter to Santa. Your letter was the whole
reason this book idea happened. I believe your kind
hearts will make such a difference in our world.

To my husband, thank you for encouraging me
through this process and telling me to go for it.

To my mom and dad, thank you
for believing that I can do anything.

To my family and friends, thank you for
all the laughs, support and love.

To the team who made this possible:
Illustrator Ylber Cërvadiku, editor Kathryn Palmer,
and my mentors, thank you for a wonderful
partnership and for bringing this book to life.

I am grateful to the Lord for this journey.
May this book bless those that read it as much as it
blessed me to write it.

Dear Santa,

How are you? My brother and I would love a surprise for Christmas. Can you also give a toy to someone who needs one?

P.S. What do you want for Christmas?

Thank you for your letter! Our head elf postman delivered it to me a few days ago. It is mighty busy here; the entire North Pole is hustling and bustling, getting ready for Christmas!

The snow is deep and we get little sleep,
as we whittle and glue making gifts just for you!

Smells of cocoa and candy canes fill the air,
as our elves make the toys, crafting each one with care.

My reindeer are groomed and all ready for flight.
And my sleigh's filling up, much to children's delight!

Boys and girls know that "St. Nick" is comin' to town!
So I'll have one last rest, and then make my way down.

As I sit by the fireside to warm up my boots,
Mrs. Claus sits beside me to patch up my suit.

She smiles at me warmly and murmurs, "My dear,
I have a question after all of these years."

"If you could give *ONE* gift, then what would it be,
for all of the children on this Christmas Eve?"

I stroke my white beard, and then touch my white head,
"Why... I'd give them the gift of REMEMBERING," I said!

This idea brought so much Christmas joy to my heart,
that I thought up a plan, and I knew I must start.

I dashed out of my chair and threw on my red coat.
I told all the elves of the letter you wrote.

"Make the toys for the kids like you always do,"
I said, "But THIS year, let us add something new!

"We'll make sparkly red & gold *REMEMBERING DUST*,
for kids to remember what's crucial—they MUST...

Think of family and friends, think of life and God's love...
and a holy, pure baby sent here from above."

To the elves I cried, "Sprinkle this dust on *each* toy,
It's magic! Made special for each girl and boy!"

So my dears, on your present there's shimmering dust.
For Santa has given you this sacred trust:

That on each Christmas day, the dust will remind
you to thank gracious God, and to always be kind.

REMEMBER, REMEMBER that one silent night,
the Christ-child was born; He was God's Holy Light.

As I lay your fine gifts underneath your bright tree,
I will pause here to thank Christ upon bended knee.

And then when you awake on the new Christmas morn,
see your dust and remember the Savior was born!

Merry Christmas,
St. Nicholas (SANTA)

Merry Christmas!

Start a New Family Tradition
Help Santa make REMEMBERING DUST!

As you prepare your home for Christmas Eve each year, don't forget to make some REMEMBERING dust for St. Nick to sprinkle on your gifts!

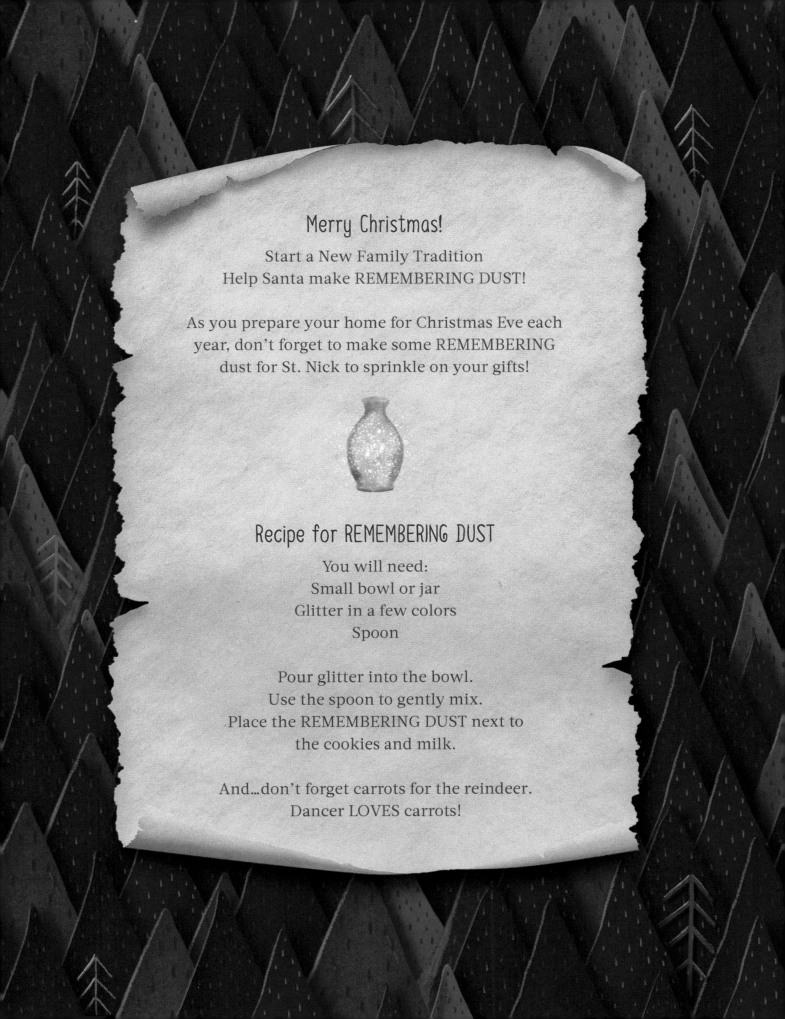

Recipe for REMEMBERING DUST

You will need:
Small bowl or jar
Glitter in a few colors
Spoon

Pour glitter into the bowl.
Use the spoon to gently mix.
Place the REMEMBERING DUST next to
the cookies and milk.

And...don't forget carrots for the reindeer.
Dancer LOVES carrots!

Did you find Santa's furry friends
hidden in the pictures?
Keep a lookout for these and other
wonderful characters in Merideth's
future books.

www.meridethtullous.com

Merideth Tullous

is a mother, wife, writer, ballet teacher and also works in a local school. She lives with her family and two goofy Goldendoodle dogs in Fort Worth, Texas. Her favorite color is neon orange and her favorite food is Cajun. Merideth would love for you to REMEMBER this story and keep an eye out for more of her creative books!

Ylber Cërvadiku

is a book illustrator, designer and painter since he was in high school in Kosovo, where he grew up and still resides with his wife and son. In his free time he bikes with his dogs, takes care of his lovely garden or even makes furniture. He was very happy to be bestowed with National Gratitude by the National Art Gallery of Kosovo. He worked really hard to create the most original images that will stick with you, hoping you will truly enjoy them and the many more to come!

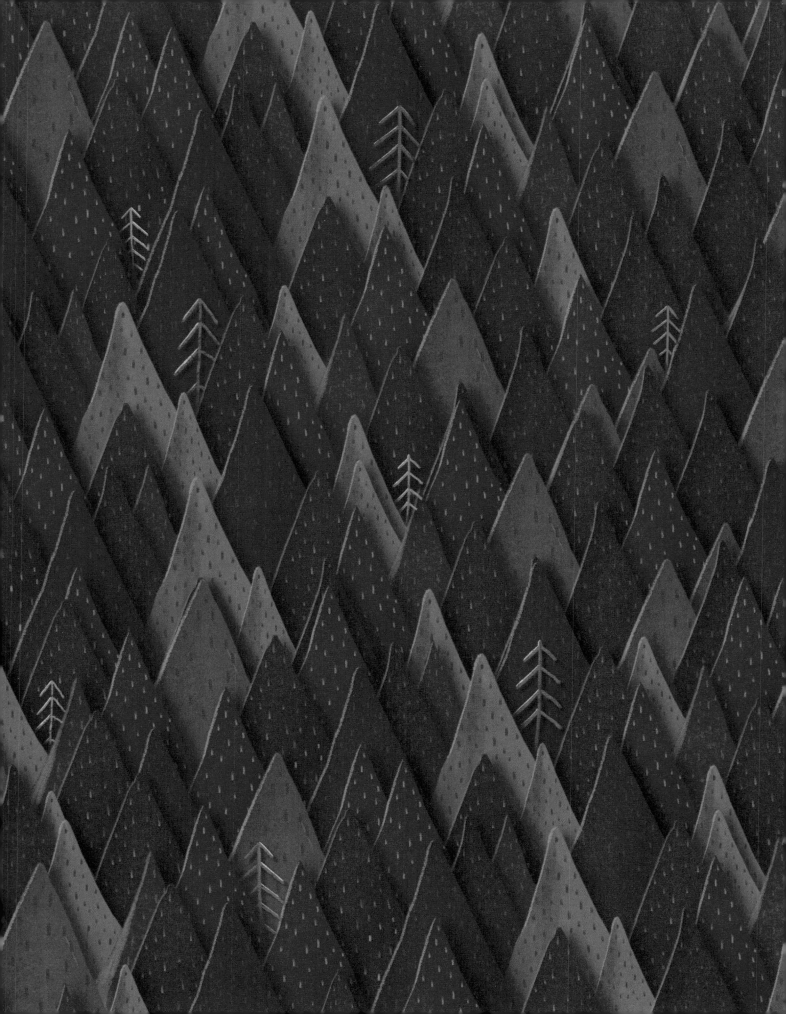

Made in the USA
Monee, IL
02 December 2020